T0127271

Dresden

Lord Berners

DRESDEN

Turtle Point Press

and

Helen Marx Books

2008

Dresden has been edited by Professor Peter Dickinson
with assistance from Dr. Mary Gifford.

Design and composition by
Wilsted & Taylor Publishing Services

Publisher's Cataloging-in-Publication
Berners, Gerald Hugh Tyrwhitt-Wilson, Baron, 1883–1950.
Dresden / Lord Berners.
p. cm.
LCCN 2007942531
ISBN 978-1-933527-15-4

Foreword

Lord Berners (1883–1950) was one of the most idio-syncratic and fascinating personalities in British mu-sic. He became a pioneer in the avant-garde when he wrote his first music whilst living in Rome as a diplo-mat during World War I; Balanchine choreographed his first two ballets and Ashton the next three; in 1931 he had the first exhibition of his paintings; in 1934 he published the first volume of his autobiography, *First Childhood*, and two years later his first novel, *The Camel* —and three more novels came out in 1941. Known as "the versatile peer," during the 1930s he increasingly gained a reputation as an eccentric, which he realised was good for publicity.

His paintings all sold and some of his novels were translated into French and Swedish: all are now back in print. But it was his music that meant the most to him and, thanks to Philip Lane and the Berners Trust, all of it is available on CD.

Berners was admired by Stravinsky, was commissioned by Diaghilev, wrote his ballet *A Wedding Bouquet* to a text by Gertrude Stein (designing the costumes and sets himself), and associated with other leading international figures in the arts. He kept a house in Rome but increasingly held court at Faringdon House (then Berkshire, now Oxfordshire) as a centre for his legendary surrealist activities such as using harmless vegetable dyes to colour his pigeons and building a useless Folly on the hill outside Faringdon against local opposition in 1935.

Between the wars he attended musical events across Europe, but World War II was a disaster that threatened everything he valued: he was at heart a European at home in various languages. Berners barely recovered from the war, although he wrote his last ballet and some film music afterwards.

His music has never been completely neglected but there was a lean period after his death in 1950 until the revival concert at the Purcell Room in 1972, with John Betjeman giving readings: this was broadcast by the BBC and led to some first recordings. There was more activity for the centenary in 1983 with London concerts, publication of songs and piano music, and a BBC Radio 3 documentary that became a book: *Lord Berners: Composer—Writer—Painter*, edited by Peter Dickinson (Boydell 2008). Through the 1990s more recordings appeared, including Berners's only opera. Berners then reached a new audience through Mark Amory's lively biography, *Lord Berners: The Last Eccentric* (Chatto & Windus, 1998), and the simultaneous reprints of the autobiographies in separate volumes and the novels bound together in *Collected Tales and Fantasies* (Turtle Point Press/Helen Marx Books, New York). The slim volume *The Château de Résenlieu* (2000) is here supplemented by *Dresden* (2008).

Gerald Berners was actually the fourteenth Baron Berners—it wasn't just a showbiz title, as his friend and colleague Constant Lambert had to explain in

America—and when he inherited in 1918 he became rich. This made him look like a dilettante, but Stravinsky recognised that if Berners was regarded as an amateur because he had no need to earn his living from the arts, it was "in the best—literal sense" and nothing he ever did was amateurish.

A wry humour pervades everything, as the brilliant orchestral *Fantaisie Espagnole* and *Three Pieces* abundantly show. His songs and piano music, too, are as full of whimsical references as those of Satie—he has been called the English Satie and the Ronald Firbank of music. Berners was not prolific, but whatever he did was stamped with his own fastidious accomplishment. He may not have been the last eccentric, but his music, writing and painting combine to make him one of the most rewarding.

Peter Dickinson

2008

Dresden

ONE

Easy conversation with the inmates of Résenlieu and the facility with which I read French books had led me to believe that I was more proficient in French than I really was.[1] Before embarking on the German language, it would have been better if I had returned to Résenlieu to perfect my French, and I should have much preferred to do so. But my mother, who had no means of judging the progress I had made, took me at my own estimate. She had heard of a good diplomatic crammer in Dresden, a Mr. Parry, and arranged for me to go to him at the beginning of 1901. I wished that I had been less boastful of my proficiency in French. I was still unsuspicious of the traps that Providence lays for boastfulness of any kind.

1. The first volume of Berners's European travels is *The Château de Résenlieu* (Turtle Point Press and Helen Marx Books, 2000).

My mother had at first intended to accompany me to Dresden, as she had accompanied me to Résenlieu, but she was unwilling to interrupt her hunting season, and I was allowed to travel out alone.

With the radiant vision of Résenlieu still fresh in my mind, I was convinced that I was going to find Germany a good deal less attractive than France, and my forebodings were confirmed by the first impressions I had of the German landscape seen through the frosted windows of my railway-carriage: interminable plains with dark masses of pine trees crawling over them like gigantic black alligators; tidy, rather smug villages and towns that looked like Christmas cards in grisaille; the general heaviness of the landscape all looked far less inspiring to the painter than the scenery of France. However, the comparison was hardly a fair one, drawn in that cold January weather, under cold/dull grey skies, the countryside flecked here and there with patches of snow that reduced everything to dull greys and browns.

I had two books to read in the train. One was *A Tramp Abroad* by Mark Twain; the other *Three Men on the Bummel* by Jerome K. Jerome.[2] These books had been recommended as being instructive of the manners and customs of the Germans. The former, a description of a Grand Tour from the point of view of an American bourgeois in the middle of the nineteenth century, seemed a little out of date, while Jerome's book was frankly too facetious to be of any real value, the chapter on Dresden, to which I eagerly turned, being devoted chiefly to an account of a tourist wanting to buy a cushion and the misunderstandings occasioned by his asking the shop-fräulein for "ein Kuss."

However there was one more serious passage about Dresden. "Dresden," it said, "is the most attractive town in Germany, a place to be lived in for a while

2. Mark Twain, pseudonym of Samuel Langhorne Clemens (1835–1910), *A Tramp Abroad* (1880). Jerome K. Jerome (1859–1927), *Three Men on the Bummel* (1900).

rather than visited. Its museums and galleries, its palaces and gardens, its beautiful and historically rich environment provide pleasure for a winter but bewilder for a week. It has not the gaiety of Paris or Vienna which quickly palls. Its charms are more solidly German and more lasting."

This didn't really get me much further, and I was obliged to evolve for myself a slightly more exciting vision of the place. All I had to go upon was Dresden china. I pictured, therefore, a town of delicate, rather ornate architecture inhabited by a people somewhat pastoral in character who, although perhaps not as gay as the inhabitants of Paris and Vienna, were nevertheless possessed of an airy, eighteenth-century elegance.

Night had fallen by the time the suburbs of Dresden appeared. The appearance of the lighted streets as the train passed along the embankment was not encouraging. They put me in mind of the outskirts of any English industrial town. Nor was I more favourably impressed by the aspect of the town itself as I drove to Frau Eberhardt's Pension in the Lindenau Strasse, a rather shabby-looking stucco house in heavy pseudo-baroque style.

Upon my ringing the bell there ensued a loud buzzing noise, such as might have been made by an angry hornet, and the door suddenly opened of its own accord. I was a little taken aback. It was my first experience of this method of controlling street doors from the interior. I felt like a traveller in a fairy tale about to be lured into the Ogre's castle, and for a moment I hesitated to enter the dark inner court. I was reassured by a substantial-looking maid-servant who appeared with a lantern and conducted me up a flight of winding stairs to the first floor. I was shown into a brilliantly lighted room where I found Frau Eberhardt, her daughter, a bald bespectacled German and two young Englishmen.

Frau Eberhardt was a plump, comfortable woman with a "friendly bust" and frizzled grey hair arranged in a low fringe on a level with her eye-brows; the daughter, Anna, was short, plain and anaemic looking; Dr. Kohlrausch, the bald, bespectacled German, was a lodger and, I discovered later, affianced to Anna. One of the young Englishmen I recognized as an Etonian. His name was Milward.[3] For athletic and social reasons he had been one of the more distinguished members of the school. Although he welcomed me in quite a friendly and condescending manner I felt a return of that awe and reverence with which such eminent persons always used to inspire me at Eton. The other Englishman, Withers by name, was, I learnt in the course of conversation, a Harrovian. Milward was extremely good-looking and Withers rather ugly. As he was a Harrovian I felt a natural superiority and was prepared to be more at my ease with him than with Milward.

3. Identified by Nancy Mitford as Sir Nevile Meyrich Henderson (1882–1942), British ambassador to Germany (1937–39) who favoured appeasing Hitler.

In spite of a general atmosphere of kindliness, I was a little embarrassed by my complete ignorance of the German language. I was also rather tired and was relieved when, after being given a cold supper of sausage, potato salad and beer, it was suggested that I might like to retire to my room, which I did after having arranged with the two Englishmen that they should take me to Mr. Parry's on the following morning.

My bedroom, which was large and comfortable-looking, was upholstered chiefly in red plush, and was rather stuffy. There was a porcelain stove in one corner that gave out a fierce heat, in which the furniture and upholstery seemed to exude a curious aroma of their own just as box hedges and fig-trees do in the heat of the sun. The room smelt also of furniture polish and stale tobacco. I tried to open one of the windows, but it was fastened in such a way as to defy my efforts. I foresaw that whatever I was going to suffer from in Frau Eberhardt's Pension, it was not going to be from cold.

The bed was strange. It was short even for my diminutive stature; the sheets were buttoned on to a thick blanket resembling in texture a horse-cloth, and there was a loose feather-lined quilt that slipped off if one made the slightest movement. It was altogether elaborate and uncomfortable. I now understood the failure of a practical joke I had once played on a German governess who had come straight from Germany and had never been in England before. On the night of her arrival I had made her an apple-pie bed. The joke, such as it was, had been a failure because she had not noticed anything at all peculiar about the arrangement. She had thought that in England beds were always made up like that.

Next morning, as soon as it was light, I went to the window in the hopes of finding that the Lindenau Strasse might be a little less depressing than it had seemed the night before. But in the daylight it was even worse, and my first impressions of the town as I walked to Mr. Parry's with Milward and Withers were distinctly discouraging. The quarter of the town through which we passed was entirely modern—that is to say that there was nothing earlier than about 1880. There was not a single building that gave me any pleasure to look at, and the inhabitants were on a par with the architecture. The women were mostly dressed in black, and the men were nearly all of them in some kind of uniform. The population seemed to be composed of widows and minor officials. The bitter cold pinched their faces and reddened their noses.

I asked Milward what Mr. Parry was like. He replied: "I think I'd better leave you to draw your own conclusions," which sounded, I thought, a little ominous.

Mr. Parry lived in the Reichenbach Strasse which, in those days, was on the very edge of the town, in fact the last completed street on that side of it. It faced a dreary slope dotted with allotment grounds. There are few aspects so cheerless as the outskirts of a modern town in the process of construction. However, when I saw Mr. Parry, the place seemed to me a suitable enough habitation for him. He was the very impersonation of gloom. His only redeeming feature was that he slightly resembled a photograph I had seen of Walter Pater.[4] He was bald and wore a heavy cavalry moustache. But his nose was considerably larger and more aquiline than Mr. Pater's. He had an anxious, haunted look. I had seldom seen a man so woe-begone in appearance. One might have imagined that he was expiating a sinful past, though, as far as I knew, he had done nothing worse than teach the classics at a preparatory school. In his present capacity, he gave instruction in all the subjects required for the diplomatic examination: German, French, Latin, Mathematics, History and Précis-writing. Into everything he taught, Mr. Parry contrived to infuse an atmosphere of melancholy—to such a degree that after a few days I began to think that I should

4. Walter Horatio Pater (1839–1894), writer and critic.

never be able to bear up under the boredom of the work involved. My despondency was increased by the discovery that I was far less advanced than any of his other pupils.

There were five of us in all. Besides Milward and Withers there were two youths who were going into the Consular Service. The general tone of Mr. Parry's Establishment was one of a rather squalid austerity. We worked in a long low classroom lit by a single window at one end, and this looked on to a blank wall. There was a deal table down the centre of the room, and there were hard kitchen chairs to sit upon. There were maps on the walls, a portrait of Queen Victoria and an enlarged photograph of Mr. Parry over the fireplace, in which there was never a fire except on very cold days.

I didn't feel much sympathy for Mr. Parry while I was under his tuition, but afterwards, when I thought of him, I felt profoundly sorry for him. So sorry in fact that I put him into the category of depressing things it is better not to think about. I succeeded in banishing him from my mind so successfully that I find it a little difficult now to resuscitate any distinct memory of him. I can remember that he lived alone in this house with one grim, elderly maidservant who called to mind the maidservant in one of Anatole France's novels: "Celle à qui personne n'ouvre la porte en souriant."[5]

Withers, who seemed to be obsessed by sex, was of the opinion that this woman was Mr. Parry's mistress. But I thought it was unlikely. Neither Mr. Parry nor his maidservant gave the impression of being disposed to any kind of amenity.

I imagine that her cooking must have been in conformity with her appearance, for Mr. Parry had never been known to invite anyone to a meal, and he complained a good deal of indigestion.

For the first few weeks I felt rather lonely. Milward

5. Anatole France (1844–1924), *Le mannequin d'osier* (1897).

and Withers, who were several years older than I was, although quite amiable, kept their distance. In my relations with them I felt rather like a lower boy at a public school. The other two young men, the embryo consuls, were uninteresting and unprepossessing and, in those days of snobbery and class distinction, I followed the lead of Milward and Withers who made it clear that people going into the diplomatic service were entitled to look down upon those destined for a consular career.

TWO

There was an old school friend of my mother's living in Dresden. My mother had written to her asking her to be kind to me. The lady's name was Miss Amy Mansfield. She was studying music, a fact of which my mother was no doubt unaware or she would have been more cautious about recommending me to her. Miss Mansfield had for many years been pegging away at her music in Dresden. As she did not appear to have any natural aptitude for music this denoted a laudable spirit of perseverance. The fact that her labours seemed to have produced but meagre results did not, however, seem to have discouraged her. She was full of enthusiasm. She was about forty. She had the rather insipid expression of a Raphael Madonna. One might have imagined that she had studied deportment in a duck pond. She waggled her bottom when she walked and looked as if, at any moment, she might be going to quack. One of her friends had christened her "The Wild Duck" after the Ibsen play that was enjoying a vogue in Dresden at the time. She would often affect a schoolgirlish espièglerie, and when anything moved her very deeply, she would shriek and clap her hands with delight. She was a great admirer of Wagner, but Brahms was her idol. Apart from certain absurdities of demeanour she was a nice gentle creature, a little bewildered by life, thoroughly kind hearted, and she made herself particularly agreeable to me. She was very popular with all the musical people in Dresden. Most of the British colony in Dresden, which at that time was a large one, seemed to be studying music or were at any rate interested in music. The atmosphere of Miss Mansfield's house was that of a kind of musical *Cranford*.[6]

6. Mrs. Elizabeth Cleghorn Gaskell (1810–65), *Cranford* (1853).

I had often thought that it would be highly enjoyable to frequent a musical world, but now that I had the opportunity of doing so, I found it a little disappointing. All these ladies took music very seriously, as seriously as in England people took sport. Unfortunately there was in most cases more earnestness than talent, and more enthusiasm was displayed about the music teachers than about music itself. The interminable discussions of the relative merits of Doctor Schwarz or Professor Weiss were just as tedious as the discussions of sport in the home circle. Occasionally I would accompany Miss Mansfield to the Music Academy where she went for her lessons. The glimpses I had of this antechamber of Parnassus filled me with depression. I was dismayed by the drabness, the squalor of the place, the grubby unattractive appearance of the music students, the peculiarly dreary sound of instruments being practised that assailed my ears as I went through the corridors. "To accomplish anything in art," Miss Mansfield used to say, "one must go through the mill." Yes, but I wanted the mill to be a picturesque, romantic affair, not a sordid-looking urban factory. Music, I felt, should exist in an environment of elegance and beauty. I thought of Haydn putting on court clothes when he composed, of Wagner in the highlands of Bavaria, of Liszt in the gardens of Villa d'Este, of Chopin in Corsica with George Sand. Much as I disliked the atmosphere of Mr. Parry's class-room, I relished just as little the idea of having to frequent such a place as the Dresden music academy. Nor was I very favourably impressed by the professional musicians I used to meet in Miss Mansfield's house. She was crazy about opera singers. There were no doubt many who were delightful and charming, but it just happened that those with whom Miss Mansfield was acquainted were arrogant and temperamental as well as elderly and physically unattractive.

Mark Twain in *A Tramp Abroad* speaks of the faithfulness of the German public to old favourites. This, I found, was very much the case in Dresden. There was in particular one elderly female Wagnerian singer who, I was told, had been remarkable in the roles of Brunnhilde and Isolde some twenty years before. It appeared that Wagner himself had thought very highly of her. I don't know how old she was now. Off the stage she might have been anything between sixty and seventy. She had the appearance of a rather disagreeable German governess. Her face wore an expression of permanent indigestion, even when she was obviously intending to be gracious. This woman was the object of a fanatic adulation both on the part of the German public and of the British colony. Schoolgirls "schwärmed" for her. Once when she appeared as Isolde after a prolonged absence, I saw a whole row of schoolgirls burst into tears. Whenever she visited Miss Mansfield or appeared elsewhere in a private capacity, she was always treated like royalty. As the embodiment of Brunnhilde or Isolde she was far from conforming to my ideal, and this was partly responsible for the decline in my adoration for Wagner.

The performances of the *Ring* to which I had looked forward with passionate eagerness left me a little disillusioned. The scenery of the *Rhinegold* was, I thought, far less effective than that of my own production in the miniature theatre at Althrey.[7] The singers, the finest Wagnerian singers in Europe, were for the most part rather elderly and unprepossessing in appearance, Brunnhilde being played by the aforesaid lady and Siegfried by a fat middle-aged tenor who looked perfectly ridiculous as he bounced about the stage in simulation of heroic youthfulness. I was physically exhausted by the length of the operas and the stuffiness of the auditorium as well as a little nauseated by the unpleasant smell emitted by the Germans. Often towards the end of an opera I would find my eyes closing. I would come to with a start and be overtaken by a sense of guilt. When I saw Miss Mansfield sitting bolt upright, all alert to the very last note, I began to wonder if perhaps after all I were not really musical.

The British colony was very much in evidence in

7. Berners's family home in Shropshire.

Dresden at that time. In the theatres, in the cafés, one heard as much English spoken as German. Thackeray observed that British colonies in continental towns brought with them all their local customs, their prejudices and their sauces. This was true of the British colony in Dresden at the beginning of the twentieth century. English society there was as strictly divided as Austrian society in Vienna. There was a good deal of snobbery, exclusiveness, class hatred—call it what you will. In the top category of society were the British Minister and his wife and any members of the aristocracy who happened to be residing in Dresden. At the Chaplain's tea-parties the Minister's wife, who was incidentally a peeress, was always given a specially valuable Meissen tea-cup, and I remember there once being a fearful row when one of the humbler guests got it by mistake. The remainder of the colony, composed chiefly of the lower upper class and upper middle class, was ruled over by a certain Mrs. Wray, who kept a finishing School for Young Ladies, a buxom, rather portentous lady whose conversational manner alternated, according to your social status, between that of interviewing parents and that of addressing pupils. She gave stately tea parties and receptions to which all the eligible were invited. She was very exclusive and a great authority on "tone." "They have a bad tone," she would say of those of whom she disapproved. At these parties Mrs. Wray was always magnificently attired, and there was nothing continental about her. She looked, as indeed she was, British to the core, the type of British matron who flourishes in the provinces, and her flounces and furbelows gave her the air of a prize cabbage at a village flower show.

A few people, enjoying a certain prominence on account of their wealth or their personalities, held themselves aloof from the British colony and were never to be seen at Mrs. Wray's parties or at those given by the Chaplain's wife. Among these was a family called Delaunay Thompson, consisting of a mother, two daughters and a son of about my age. The Delaunay Thompsons were reputed to be immensely rich. An impression of wealth was conveyed by expensive-looking clothes and a haughty bearing. They were generally described as looking "stuck up." I used to see them at the opera, occupying a large box on the first tier or strolling magnificently in the foyer surrounded by German officers, attracted perhaps by the "dots" of the Miss Delaunay Thompsons. They resided at the Hotel Belle Vue, the smartest and most expensive of the Dresden hotels, and when I went to the restaurant of the hotel I used to see them dining in state amid a bevy of obsequious waiters. These people became for me a sort of social ideal. I longed to know them, to sit in their box at the opera, to stroll with them in the foyer, to dine with them in state at the Hotel Belle Vue. I should have liked to have it said of me: "He is an intimate friend of the Delaunay Thompsons."

But, alas! it was not to be. I could discover no possible means of contact with them.

Mrs. Wray said that they were merely vulgar industrialists from Birmingham. However, I fancy that if the Miss Delaunay Thompsons had been at Mrs. Wray's Finishing School she might have given a different version of their origin.

Then there was a Miss Daphne Craig. Here amorous rather than social ambitions were involved. Miss Craig was an extremely beautiful young woman, always wonderfully dressed in the height of fashion. She was about the only person in Dresden who wore what was known in those days as "Paris frocks." She was tall and graceful, altogether a most ravishing creature. She was supposed to be "fast." Mrs. Wray spoke of her with disapproval; but I don't imagine she would have been averse to making her acquaintance had she been given an opportunity to do so.

Miss Daphne Craig, like the Delaunay Thompsons, "kept herself to herself." She was often to be seen at the opera, generally in the company of some of the leading opera singers on their off nights, much to the envy of the English schoolgirls. I used to worship Miss Craig from afar. My heart would beat violently whenever I passed her in the foyer or met her in the streets—unlike the Delaunay Thompsons she was occasionally to be seen walking in the streets.

This Dante and Beatrice relationship was on the whole perhaps the most satisfactory, for, had I been introduced to her, I should, at that period of my life, have been far too shy to do anything but gape, and she didn't look the sort of young woman who would be likely to take much trouble about a timid youth.

At the age of seventeen, in unsatisfactory neutral periods, when I was not dominated by any particular personal relationship, such people as these, as well as certain characters in fiction, often used to play a more important part in my life than the people I knew and consorted with.

After leaving Dresden I never saw or heard of either the Delaunay Thompsons or Miss Daphne Craig again. The latter I believe, married a German officer and disappeared into Darkest Germany.

Apart from Frau Eberhardt, her daughter, Doktor Kohlrausch and such friends and relations who came to the house, I didn't know very many Germans. Nevertheless it was possible to get a fairly good impression of the manners and customs of the Germans, of the Saxons at any rate, by observing them in the streets, in the cafés and theatres. One objectionable trait I noticed was the way in which they managed, in the foyer and in the corridors of the opera house, to bump into one as they passed, even if there was plenty of room on the other side. At first I took it to be a manifestation of a dislike for foreigners, a crude form of xenophobia. Later I came to understand that it was due to an inherent lack of proportion, to an inability to judge distances, both material and spiritual. For the same thing happened in social relationships. They were always bumping into you and appeared to be almost deliberately regardless of the direction you were trying to take.

Another thing that I found rather unattractive

about the Germans was their excessive regard for law and order. In England those not directly concerned generally adopted an attitude of neutrality in the face of some minor breach of the law. Here everyone seemed to be instinctively on the side of the police. If you trod on the grass in a public garden, if you took your hands off the handlebars of your bicycle, if you walked with your stick or your umbrella under your arm, officious citizens would shout at you: "Das ist verboten!" Indeed, it was the minor contraventions that seemed to incur the greatest odium. There was a legend that a man who had thrown his wife and children out of a top storey window had been charged firstly with throwing things out of a window, and secondly, with murder!

Although, as a result of my experience at Résenlieu and in Dresden I was inclined to compare the Germans, in most respects, unfavourably with the French, I was forced to admit that there was a greater sense of domestic comfort in Germany than in France, where style and elegance predominated.

The famous German Gemütlichkeit! It was often impressed upon me by Frau Eberhardt and her friends that there was no exact counterpart of the word in any other language. In fact the Germans were the sole proprietors of Gemütlichkeit. Certainly domestic life, as I knew it in Dresden, had a very definite charm. At the end of a long afternoon spent in Mr. Parry's dank and gloomy classroom, it was very pleasant to get back to the plush and fug of Frau Eberhardt's Wohnzimmer, to her placid amiability and the excellent if rather stodgy food which resulted from her frequent incursions into the kitchen. "Heute abend haben wir Kartoffelpuffer" (we have potato cakes for supper) she would announce in confidential tones.

Occasionally there took place a ceremony called Kaffeekränzchen when a number of ladies would invade the house, sit in a circle and consume coffee and gossip. For these events a special cake would be provided, a Baumkuchen, a sort of erection that resembled a tree trunk with short branches sticking out of it, made of a heavy rolled sponge-cake coated with sugar. There was a decidedly Christmasy air about these entertainments.

I also enjoyed the large comfortable cafés where one could sit at tables drinking chocolate and listening to classical music played by a really excellent orchestra.

Yet, from an apparent kindliness of disposition, an amiable cosiness, there would, from time to time, emerge rather ominous indications of cruelty and brutal cynicism. Frau Eberhardt herself was eminently gemütlich, but she would at moments give vent to quite hair-raising sentiments, especially with regard to some foreign nation, the French, the Italians and, I've no doubt if I had not been present, the English. In general also I noticed a latent admiration for "frightfulness." It would be said of someone how good, how gentle he was and then, with an air of final appreciation, "Kann auch sehr unangenehm sein" (can also make himself extremely disagreeable).

Of course, at the time, I didn't know about schizophrenia—even today[8] the word is not in the Oxford Dictionary—but schizophrenia was evidently what many of the Germans were suffering from, a complaint that, together with their exaggerated reverence for law and order, a will to regimentation, has caused them, even more than a natural bellicosity to which other nations are equally prone, to be responsible for most of the disasters that have overtaken Europe.

8. In the later 1940s.

THREE

Milward and Withers began to relax their rather exclusive attitude towards me. They had come to realize, perhaps, that I was more worthy of their attention than they had believed me to be at first. This change of heart made a good deal of difference to my life in Dresden. It was heartening to my amour propre to be promoted from the status of lower boy to a relationship of equality, though it was hardly one of equality with regard to Milward. I was still in the hero-worshipping stage, and this paragon of charm and beauty soon took the place previously occupied by Longworth and Deniston in the scale of my affections.[9] Young men of the Milward type are usually responsive to the flattery of admiration, and his re-

9. See Berners's *First Childhood* (1934) and *A Distant Prospect* (1945).

sponse to mine was adequate enough to cause me a great deal of happiness. In my early youth I was apt to be more impressed by people of elegance and social brilliancy than, much as I loved music and literature, by prominent figures in the latter fields. And, in any case, people like Milward were, at that time, more within my range.

Withers and Milward saw even less Germans than I did and, except at meal times, they were very seldom in the house. They had made a large circle of English and American friends, most of whom would not, I imagine, have been approved of by Mrs. Wray—neither would Mrs. Wray have been approved of by them. They were, on the whole, rather a rowdy lot, but of a quite inoffensive kind of rowdiness, the result of youth and high spirits and occasionally of a lack of breeding. I don't know what exactly they were doing in Dresden. They were certainly not studying music, neither did they contribute very much to good will among the nations.

One of the ringleaders of this group was a very

good-looking young woman called Miss Sylvia Sparks. She might be described as a less expensive edition of Miss Daphne Craig. Milward was very much in love with her and, in the measure that my intimacy with him increased, so did his confidences with regard to Miss Sylvia Sparks. It required all the strength of my devotion to enable me to put up with the perpetual unburdening of his passion. In any case it was rather a hopeless passion, for Miss Sparks was engaged to be married to a young man who was shortly coming to Dresden. He was a bank clerk, I believe. When he did eventually appear he proved to be a rather vulgar creature and considerably less attractive in every way than Milward. I couldn't help thinking that it was a little pusillanimous of Milward not to have succeeded in achieving—at least something. But Miss Sparks, for all her reputation for "fastness," was at heart a highly respectable middle-class young woman, and she was perhaps sensible enough to realise that, in view of the difference of their social position, there was nothing very solid to be hoped for from Milward's direction. So she flirted outrageously with him and stuck to her bank clerk.

Milward had written a poem, a very bad one, dedicated to Miss Sparks, and asked me to set it to music. My first introduction to Miss Sparks took place on the occasion of my playing to her what I had written. The music, I fear, was not much better than the poem. However, she professed to be enchanted with it. She had a fashionable leaning to the arts but knew nothing whatever about them.

At first Miss Sparks terrified me. I was disconcerted by the vulgarity of her manners combined with such a very alluring appearance. I knew that I had nothing whatever in common with her and felt in her presence a bit of a muff. I was also a little impressed by her not responding more gratefully to my paragon's attentions.

However, if only on Milward's account, I determined to persevere and try to win from her, if possible, a little more respect. I would indulge from time to time in conversational obscenities, which I fancied would let her see that I was not quite such a muff as she might imagine. But, instead of impressing her as I had hoped, they merely shocked her, and she told Milward that she didn't think his friend had a very nice mind. I never really succeeded in making much headway with Miss Sylvia Sparks.

Withers, who was a born roué, was a little contemptuous of Milward's amorous life. He said of him that in his love affairs he was more like Lord Byron than Don Juan, romantic rather than operative. It was Lady Blessington, I believe, who said that Byron had the reputation of being an indifferent lover. However, as I believed at the time in Byron's traditional label, I was a little surprised at Withers' distinction. He also complained that Milward never went with tarts. Withers, on the other hand, constantly did and was always getting venereal disease in consequence.[10]

10. Berners crossed out this paragraph in the typescript. Such discretion is no longer necessary.

Withers was right in saying that Milward was romantic. He was one of the most romantic young men I have ever known—not only in his relation with women. He lived in a world of romantic make-believe. Whenever he went to a play he would, for days afterwards, see himself in the role of the hero. He was a strange mixture of naiveté and sophistication. It seems strange now that I should have ever believed him to be, as I did in those days, a consummate man of the world. However, he was a man of his own world, and it was a world that never expanded. Perhaps that is why, in later life, he was a failure as an Ambassador.

At the age of nineteen he had certainly a very attractive personality, and I think he was better than he ever was subsequently. There are many Englishmen who are at their zenith round about the age of twenty and afterwards cease to develop. I used to think that he was very intelligent. Most of us, I believe, are as intelligent at the age of twenty than we ever become later, and it is the manner in which experience is assimilated that makes the difference. It is the digestion of experience that makes us better and wiser men. There must have been something a little sticky about Milward's psychological metabolism because, when I met him again some thirty years later, I found him exactly the same as when I had known him in Dresden—only a little less physically attractive.

FOUR

I made a more speedy progress in reading German than I did in speaking it, and soon I was able to read German books with a certain facility. Nietzsche was one of my first discoveries.[11] My approach to him was from a musical rather than philosophical angle. I had heard one of Miss Mansfield's musical friends speak bitterly of Nietzsche, having been outraged by his recently published attack on Wagner. She said that anyhow Nietzsche had gone mad and Wagner hadn't— which seemed to her a conclusive argument in favour of the latter. I immediately bought *Der Fall Wagner* and was enthralled by it. As often happened with me, my enjoyment of the book was heightened by my not

11. Friedrich Wilhelm Nietzsche (1844–1900), *Der Fall Wagner* (1888).

quite understanding a good deal of it. I was a little surprised that Wagner should be denounced as a "decadent." I had always imagined, as did apparently in later times the Nazis, that he was the apotheosis of Nordic vigour and virility. That Wagner was a bit of a cabotin, yes![12] The appearance of the actor in music. But that his music was a poison, a public danger, of that I was not wholly convinced. What appealed to me most in the book was the treatment of certain absurdities of which I was already half aware—particularly the passage relating to the third act of Siegfried where Wagner suddenly realises that there have been no female characters on the stage. As all the heroines were at the moment otherwise engaged, what does he do? He summons Erda, the oldest woman on earth. Up she comes out of a trap-door and, after having fulfilled her function, down she goes again. "Return to your slumbers, ancient Grandmama."

12. A show-off.

I also liked the comments on Wagner's "redemption" craze—how "alte verdorbene Frauenzimmer" (old debauched baggages) like Kundry prefer to be redeemed by chaste young men, and how innocent saints like Elizabeth have a predilection for saving interesting sinners. I thought these things were very funny, but they were more concerned with Wagner's philosophy and stagecraft than with his music. I think, on the whole, *Der Fall Wagner* was less responsible for the waning of my Wagner enthusiasm than my actual experience of Wagner operas on the stage and the elderly prima donna who played all the principal roles.

Also sprach Zarathustra was, I had heard, Nietzsche's best book or, if not his best, the most famous. I acquired a very handsome copy of it bound in sham leather, and its possession gave me the wildest pleasure, a slightly priggish pleasure I fear. I displayed the book proudly on my table, and sometimes I took it to a café and would read it ostentatiously with the idea that people might say of me: "What a very cultivated young Englishman to be reading *Also sprach Zarathustra* in a café!" The pleasure it gave me was also of a slightly fetishist character. I liked the look of the lettering and the quasi-biblical lay out. But whether I understood it is another matter. Milward took it up, one day, from my table and said: "Good God, do you mean to say you understand this?"

"Up to a point," I admitted.

"Well then," he said, selecting a passage at random, "what does this mean?"

Luckily it was fairly simple and I was able to explain it. But it had been touch and go.

I read other German authors besides Nietzsche, but in a more perfunctory way, with the examination looming in the background. I kept a note-book into which I transcribed every word and phrase that I thought might come in useful for examination purposes, and I remember the joy with which, when the examination period was over, I was able to read foreign books solely for pleasure without having to bother about the new words and phrases I came upon.

In a similarly perfunctory manner I used to make a point of having some conversation every day with Frau Eberhardt and Anna. Of these conversations hardly a memory remains, no doubt because they never said anything worth remembering. I do, however, recollect that there was a good deal of talk about food and that Frau Eberhardt once said of some beauty spot or some place of historical interest they had visited: "That was the place where we had those excellent veal cutlets" (herrliche Kalbskoteletten), and that once at a restaurant she had said to the waiter who was serving her: "Es ist doch nicht genug" (it is still not enough) a phrase, I thought, that would have made a good text for a Bach motet.

FIVE

Some excitement was caused in the British colony by the arrival in Dresden of an eccentric peer, the Marquis of Anglesey, and by the announcement that he was going to appear at one of the principal music halls. Since marquises in those days still enjoyed a certain veneration, particularly among the British colony in Dresden, this was considered very eccentric indeed. Mrs. Wray complained that Lord Anglesey was "letting down" the peerage, and Miss Mansfield was of the opinion that no Englishmen ought to go and see him disgrace himself. It would have been bad enough if he had been going to take the part of Siegfried at the opera house—but to appear at a music hall!

I had heard that Lord Anglesey had previously appeared in other continental music halls, and that all he did was to show himself on the stage attired in the family jewels. It didn't sound to me a very exciting performance; however, in spite of Miss Mansfield's injunction, I was determined to go and see it.

If not exactly exciting it was decidedly a strange "turn." It came between that of a lady with performing pigeons and a company of acrobats. The theatre was darkened. There was a roll on the drums and the curtain went up on Lord Anglesey clad in a white silk tunic, a huge diamond tiara on his head, glittering with necklaces, brooches, bracelets and rings. He stood there for a few minutes, motionless, without any mannequin gestures of display. Then the curtain went down again. No applause followed, only an animated buzz of conversation. The German audience seemed a little disconcerted by this manifestation of British eccentricity. I may say that German audiences even in the music halls were extraordinarily disciplined and well-behaved. Once at the Dresden opera a new tenor, appearing for the first time in the role of

Lohengrin, missed his footing on stepping out of the swan-boat and fell headlong on the stage. His shield and helmet were restored to him by members of the chorus, and the performance was resumed in perfect silence. There was not the sound of the faintest chuckle. Lord Anglesey, I thought, had got off lightly. Imagine the reception of such a display by an English music hall audience. The press treated the matter with similar restraint. The notices merely commented on the magnificence of the jewels. German propaganda had not yet taken up the subject of British decadence. In later years poor Lord Anglesey would no doubt have been accused by his compatriots of being in the pay of the German government and of being employed by them to bring the British nation into disrepute.

SIX

After this the two most interesting events were my discovery of Richard Strauss and the commotion caused in Mr. Parry's establishment by a caricature.

My enthusiasm for Wagner had, as I have said, considerably abated. I was musically at a loose end and returned for a time to Chopin. I practised assiduously the Preludes, but I had never acquired a proper piano technique and, although my performance might perhaps have impressed the ignorant, it would not have passed muster with a connoisseur.

One day I went to a concert and heard Richard Strauss's symphonic poem *Till Eulenspiegel*. I was fairly bowled over by it. My subsequent passion for Richard Strauss equalled if not exceeded my former passion for Wagner. These early musical enthusiasms of mine were something akin to falling in love. When first

Richard Strauss swam into my ken I could think of little else. The sight of a Richard Strauss score in a shop window was like meeting the beloved one at a street corner. Although I could at that time hardly read an orchestral score I got hold of *Don Juan* and would pore over it in a state of wild excitement. The mere printed notes seemed to radiate a mystical rapture, even greater than the actual sounds when I heard them in the concert hall. And as on the occasion of my first passion for Wagner, when I became fired with the idea of writing an opera, I was now bent on composing a symphonic poem. My knowledge of musical technicalities was hardly more advanced than it had been on the former occasion. However, I did at least realise that some knowledge of orchestration might be necessary. I determined to study orchestration.

Miss Mansfield whom I consulted said that the best teacher of orchestration in Dresden was an elderly composer, Professor Kretschmer, who had written several operas that were very rarely performed.

She seemed a little surprised that I should wish to embark on orchestration before I had mastered the more elementary branches of music. But she was pleased that I should want to study anything connected with music and, being acquainted with Professor Kretschmer, arranged for me to have an interview with him.

Whatever may have been Professor Kretschmer's merits as a composer, at all events he looked like a very distinguished one, and in addition he was a very charming old gentleman. He reminded me a little of Monsieur de Rosen, only he was altogether a more imposing figure. His longish grey hair was brushed back in the same way from his forehead, and he had the same sort of drooping moustache. In the house he always wore a black velvet coat edged with braid. His study, where I had my lessons, was a most inspiring room with faded laurel wreaths tied up with scarlet ribbons on the walls; there was a huge grand piano, a mask of Beethoven and bookcases filled with scores and books on music. I thought that any one possessing such a room could not fail to be a genius. Professor Kretschmer's ambience was an effective antidote to the depression caused by my visits to the Music Academy, and all my musical ambitions flowered once more. Diplomacy faded for the moment into the background, and I almost made up my mind to brave parental displeasure and devote my life to music. The Professor didn't seem to be at all embarrassed by my comparative ignorance of other musical technicalities. That was not his concern. His duty was to teach me orchestration.

I had exactly three lessons from Professor Kretschmer. They were brought to an end by the untimely arrival of my mother in Dresden as a consequence of the affair of the caricature which I will now recount.[13]

One evening as we left Mr. Parry's class-room, Withers drew a life-size caricature of Mr. Parry's

13. Berners's letters to his mother suggest that he had at least twelve lessons.

head on the blackboard. Withers's draughtsmanship was not particularly expert, but Mr. Parry's features were not very difficult to reproduce; a bald head, a bushy moustache and a large beaky nose (in this instant enlivened by a pendent drop) were all that was necessary to ensure a likeness.

Thinking no more about the matter Milward and I went that evening to a performance of Hauptmann's *Die versunkene Glocke* at the Residenz Theater.[14] When we came out after the first act we found Mr. Parry waiting for us in the foyer. (I never discovered how he had managed to track us down.) He seemed very agitated.

"I thought it would be as well," he said, "to strike while the iron is hot," and he followed up this forcible metaphor by an almost hysterical outburst about the caricature he had found on the blackboard. He

14. Gerhart Hauptmann (1862–1946), *The Sunken Bell* (1897).

seemed to be convinced that it was I who had been its perpetrator. A spirit of fourth-form heroics got the better of my sense of justice as well as of my pride as an artist, and I never denied it. Next day he sent a telegram to my mother complaining of my behaviour. Hence my mother's arrival in Dresden.[15]

Her state of mind was balanced between distress at my lapse of decorum and the pleasure of an unexpected continental trip chargeable to her sense of duty, the hunting season now being over. By the time my mother had arrived, Mr. Parry had cooled down somewhat, and I think he was now a little ashamed of having made such a fuss. As soon as the trouble had been disposed of, my mother settled down to enjoy herself in Dresden. We visited the galleries and the museums together and I took her to the opera. The

15. Berners's mother's diary for 5 March 1901: "Heard from Mr. Parry Gerald had been very rude to him." 25 March: "Saw Mr. Parry for over an hour!"

Wagner season was over and nothing very interesting was being performed at the time. We went to see an opera called *Nausicaa*, part of a Homeric tetralogy by an indifferent composer, Bungert by name, who was setting out to rival Wagner on Hellenic lines.[16] It was a long, boring opera, and my mother didn't enjoy it. She said she found it a strain to attend to the music and what was taking place on the stage at the same time. Although in this case neither was very much worth attending to, I suppose it is a reproach that might be brought against any opera. Anyhow we did not go to the opera again.

We spent a few days in Saxon Switzerland at a small hotel on the Bastei. Milward, by whom my mother was very favourably impressed, accompanied us, and it was no doubt due to his presence, as well as to the wonderful May weather, that this was perhaps the happiest time of my Dresden period.

16. August Bungert (1845–1915), *Nausicaa* (1901).

Saxon Switzerland, I imagine, remains today very much as it was at the beginning of the century. There may be a few more hotels, a few more notice boards. Those "singular rock-formations," as Baedeker describes them, rising up on both sides of the Elbe, looking like a landscape painted by Patinir (perhaps it actually was Saxon Switzerland that he painted—I don't know.)[17] There were Wagnerian aspects too, Walhalla-like peaks, slabs of rock where Brunnhilde might have reposed encircled by flames, precipitous rocky paths leading down through wooded slopes to the Elbe, where at any moment you might expect to see Mime or Alberich popping up out of a rocky cavity. I did some sketching while we were there but without much success. The scenery was too like folklore, too märchenhaft, to suit my style, and my capacity for figure drawing was not sufficient to enable me to embellish it, Boecklin-fashion, with Germanic nymphs,

17. Joachim Patinir (c. 1480–1524), Netherlands.

fauns and kobolds. A few days after our return to Dresden my mother went back to England. She had brought her maid Dawson with her. Dawson's comments on Germany and the Germans were not as enlightening as usual. She said she thought Dresden was a dull town and that the Germans dressed badly and looked as if they drank too much beer.

Before leaving, my mother had arranged that I should stay on for another month with Mr. Parry (the caricature having finally sunk into oblivion) and then go to a family she had heard of in the Harz Mountains.

Milward was returning to England at the end of the month to go to the famous diplomatic crammer, Scoones, and as it was his company that made my life in Dresden more or less tolerable, I welcomed the change that was before me.

Although I have often been told that Dresden is a delightful town I was never able to appreciate its charm. It may have been because I lived in an ugly modern quarter which I was obliged to traverse every time I wanted to get to a more interesting section of the town. The Saxons appeared to me to be an unattractive race, unprepossessing, unfriendly, gross in appearance and manners. With the exception of a few members of the foreign colony, one seldom saw a good-looking or well-dressed person in the streets. The place was pervaded by an atmosphere of heaviness, drabness, an absence of vitality. Mr. Parry's establishment accentuated the gloom.

THE HARZ[18]

In the first week of June 1901 I left Dresden for the Harz. Frau Eberhardt had been loud in her praise of the country and had continually assured me how much I should enjoy being there. She said it was by far

18. German mountains and now a national park southeast of Hanover.

the most beautiful part of Germany but, as she didn't seem to have travelled very extensively in her own native land, I was inclined to suspect that her opinion might be due to the fact that the Harz was one of the few places she had visited. As a preparation for my coming experience I read Heine's *Harzreise*, which heightened my expectations far more than Frau Eberhardt's testimony in its favour.[19]

The house of the "Förstmeister" Müller was my destination. The title of Förstmeister aroused anticipations of a sort of Robin Hood–like character which were to some extent confirmed by the appearance of the Förstmeister himself, when he met me at the station of Harzburg in a rustic-looking conveyance drawn by two spirited horses. He was a tall huntsman-like fellow dressed in a pale green uniform with dark green lapels and cuffs and a green brush in his hat. He seemed to be rather a stupid man, but his

19. Heinrich Heine (1797–1856), *Travel Pictures* (1826–31).

manner was authoritative, and stupid people with authoritative manners have always impressed me.

The Försthaus was about five or six miles from Harzburg. We drove through a very pretty valley, thickly wooded, but not, I was pleased to notice, with pine trees. The vegetation was composed for the most part of beeches and oaks. The house was situated on a spot where the valley widened out into a large open space covered with heather and rough grass through which there ran a stream about forty yards from the house. A neat little garden separated the road from the house which was a long, low building of whitish, roughcast stone covered with lattice-work espaliered with pear trees and creepers. The romantically rural aspect of the place delighted me after five months spent in a town.

The Frau Förstmeister was a woman of rather austere appearance. She had dark, smooth hair done up in a bun behind. Her features were pleasing but rather insignificant. She had one of those faces that have been described as "once seen never remembered." Although she appeared to be amiably disposed, the general impression she made was one of stiffness and angularity. She looked a little like a schoolmistress and it was, in fact, she who was responsible for the educational side of the establishment.

There were two small boys aged about nine and ten whose names were Ernst and Heinrich.

I was given a fairly spacious room overlooking the garden. It was barely furnished, and the floor was carpetless. It looked as if it might have been cold in winter, but it contained the usual German stove and I imagined that the usual German fug could have been achieved if necessary.

We had a nice substantial tea with plenty of cream, butter and jam in a little arbour in the garden. I soon discovered that the Förstmeister and his wife were, from my own particular point of view, not very intelligent people. That is to say that they took no interest whatever in music, art or literature. However, they seemed to be sensible and agreeable and I felt that I was going to be happy with them, if a little dull.

I was in no doubts as to the charm of the surrounding country. The two little boys were deputed to take me for a walk and show me the chief spots of interest in the immediate vicinity—the Waldmühle, the waterfall, the Philosopher's Walk. The Germans have a habit of designating certain places as officially interesting and providing them with observation towers, restaurants and notice boards so that they can go straight into Baedeker without further ado. The country was less mountainous here than in other parts of the Harz; however, it made up for what it lacked in dramatic grandeur by a homely, intimate attractiveness.

The valley continued for several miles, flanked by high wooded hills. A little rushing stream flowed down the centre of it, widening out here and there into stretches that might almost be dignified by the name of river. On its banks lay the little village of Immenthal, a modest summer resort, of which most of the houses were built of wood. It had a picturesque church and a friendly-looking creeper-clad Gasthaus, gay with window-boxes and striped awnings. The atmosphere of the countryside was that of an illustration by Ludwig Richter whose work Baedeker tells us is "typically German and homely as are the fairy tales of Grimm."[20]

Every morning after breakfast I had a German lesson with Frau Müller. In spite of her somewhat scholastic appearance her scholastic methods were quite as unprofessional as had been those of O'Kerrins. But unlike Madame O'Kerrins she had no sense of humour and, whatever you may say, a sense of humour is far from being a defect in a teacher. Also, apart from considerations of grammar and vocabulary, her opinions on almost every other subject were totally devoid of interest. I tried to get her to explain

20. Adrian Ludwig Richter (1803–84).

to me certain parts of the *Harzreise* that I had been unable to understand, but she was not very helpful. She might have been excused for failing to elucidate the allusions to local Göttingen gossip in the first chapter, but I found that I was as well able to cope with the poetical and humorous passages as she was. She seemed on the whole a little mistrustful of Heine: she was inclined to be mistrustful of both sentiment and irony wherever they appeared. With Nietzsche she would have nothing to do. She said that *Also sprach Zarathustra* could be of no earthly use to me for examination purposes. Here she was right no doubt. So our reading was confined to rather dreary historical books and the local newspaper.

Frau Müller was, I discovered, of Prussian origin, and from veiled insinuations I gathered that she had married slightly beneath her. However, the Förstmeister looked the more distinguished of the two. He was very seldom in the house. He was intensively occupied by his forestal duties. I should say that he was thoroughly efficient in his profession. But from a social point of view he was distinctly impersonal, quite as impersonal as Mr. Oxney had been at Eton.

The two little boys, Ernst and Heinrich, who had seemed, at first sight, to be comparatively harmless, turned out to possess in embryo all the nastiest characteristics of the German race. They were alternately arrogant and cringing. They used to bully the servants and the smaller village children, but they would collapse and whine if there were the slightest sign of retaliation or firmness of character. A harsh word would reduce them to respectful compliance. I was relieved to hear that they were going away to a cadet school in a few weeks' time.

The Müller family appeared to have an almost religious veneration for the Kaiser. They didn't seem to be religious in any other respect and I imagined that, in their hierarchy, God must have occupied very definitely a back seat. Frau Eberhardt had never appeared to have any very great respect for the Kaiser. I had even heard some rather ribald jokes made about him. With the Müllers it was a very different matter, and I felt that it was injudicious even to mention the Kaiser, just as it was a little unwise, in the home circle in England, to mention God.

The Müllers extended their veneration to all the members of the imperial family, and the fact that two of the young princes were at the cadet school to which the boys were going converted it into a sort of paradise to which they were looking forward with the most ardent anticipation.

After a fortnight I was beginning to have a premonition of approaching boredom. Luckily the situation was relieved by the arrival of Onkel Peter.

Onkel Peter was the elder brother of the Frau Förstmeister. From what I gathered he was not particularly popular either with his sister or with the Förstmeister. They said of him: "Er ist ein wenig verrückt" (he is a little mad), and I don't imagine that his presence would have been so cheerfully tolerated if he had not been fairly wealthy and a Graf. He was unmarried and I suppose there were definite hopes of inheritance.

Onkel Peter was a man of about fifty. He was rather fat and had a round, ruddy, clean-shaven face and closely cropped hair that stood up in bristles, and he wore very large spectacles. He had a slightly Prussian appearance, but this was deceptive—a sheep in wolf's clothing. He was very different in character from his sister, and was vastly more intelligent than either of the Müllers. He was obviously well read and took a keen interest in literature and art.

The very first evening he started talking to me about Voltaire, which seemed to embarrass and irritate the Müllers. I think he expected to embarrass me as well, and he seemed a little astonished to find that I did happen to know something about Voltaire and had read *Candide*.[21] For a German and a man of such elephantine proportions he was singularly nimble-

21. Voltaire, pseudonym of François-Marie Arouet (1694–1778), *Candide* (1759).

witted, and when he teased the Förstmeister, which he did pretty frequently, the process was rather like the onslaughts of a large butterfly on a small cabbage. I think Onkel Peter was a little sorry for his sister, but he had given her up as hopeless. As for Ernst and Heinrich, he certainly had no very great affection for them. He once confided to me that he considered that they combined the aggressiveness of mosquitoes with the humility of worms. He seemed indeed to be so little in harmony with the entire Müller family that I wondered why he ever came to stay with them. It must have been that he had a very dutiful regard for family ties.

I made great friends with Onkel Peter. We used to go for long walks together, and he would discourse to me on literature, music and life in general. We didn't walk very fast. Onkel Peter used to puff and pant a good deal, and he would frequently stop and mop his brow with a large purple silk handkerchief.

He was pleased with me for liking Heine and

Nietzsche. "They are the two finest writers of German prose that we possess," he said, "and can be compared for the brilliance and the clarity of their style to certain French authors." (He had a great admiration for Voltaire, Renan and Anatole France.) "But," he added, "pay no attention to Nietzsche's philosophy. It is nonsense."

I was puzzled. "But surely—isn't Nietzsche a good philosopher?"

"He is a wit and a poet and that is more than sufficient. In any case philosophy is very tiresome and merely consists in saying things that most people hardly think worth while saying, in longwinded and incomprehensible language."

I was glad to hear this as I had been rather discouraged by the few incursions I had made into the realm of philosophy.

On musical questions I was less in sympathy with him. He took no interest in any composer later than Beethoven. When I mentioned Richard Strauss to him he snorted and said: "I suppose it is the kind of stuff that impresses young people nowadays. But it won't do."

Onkel Peter's unreasonableness about modern music led me to wonder if he might not perhaps be a little unreliable about other matters. I often wished afterwards that I had been older at the time and more advanced in my culture, so that I could have appreciated more wholeheartedly the things he used to say to me.

The Frau Förstmeister was, I think, pleased that I held so much conversation with her brother, as it relieved her, to a certain extent, of her educational duties, as well as of the company of Onkel Peter and myself. I don't fancy that she felt any very great affection for me, and the Förstmeister, I was sure, rather despised me for not being more interested in forestal matters and in more active outdoor pursuits. Once when I was driving with him he said to me: "Can you drive?" "Of course," I replied. He handed the reins to me, but German horses didn't seem to respond to the reins in the same way that English horses did, and I drove him into a ditch. Another time he gave me his gun to shoot at a falcon and I missed it, which was a great source of joy to the two little boys who continually referred thereafter to the occasion when "der Herr Engländer hatte an einem Falken vorbeigeschossen."

I was grateful to Onkel Peter for saying to them one day in the playfully sarcastic tones he always adopted when speaking to them: "You nasty little creatures, I think your father would love you better if you were horses or roe-deer."

The more I saw of Onkel Peter the more I liked him. But there was no doubt that he was a little crazy, and there was perhaps some justification for what the Müllers had said of him. There were rather alarming moments when his brain seemed to have got stuck in a groove and he would continue to repeat some phrase or other ad infinitum. I remember one morning when it was raining he sat in the porch with the house-cat, which was also named Peter, chanting to it for nearly an hour:

> Peter, Peter, Peterlein.
> Peterlein, es regnet.
> Peter, Peter, Peterlein.
> Peterlein, es regnet.

THE BROCKEN

As a treat for Ernst and Heinrich, before they left for the cadet school, an excursion to the Brocken was arranged. Onkel Peter, after having at first protested against the expedition, finally decided to go with us, for which I was glad as I foresaw his participation would preclude too strenuous an outing.

We left early in the morning. The train journey took several hours, and we arrived at about ten o'clock at a little village (I have forgotten its name) in a valley just below the Brocken. Here the Müllers got out to make the ascent on foot—it took about two hours—while Onkel Peter and I continued in the train and were landed nearly at the summit.

There are two excellent descriptions of an ascent of the Brocken, both by poets. One by Heine in the *Harzreise*. The other by Coleridge. The two accounts are very different. Coleridge describes with a wealth of poetic detail the scenery observed during the ascent and the descent of the mountain, but of the Brocken itself he says practically nothing. Except for a short poem in which he speaks of his longing for England and the ubiquity of God, he passes it over in silence.[22] Heine, on the other hand, gives an elaborate account of the scenes of jollity and dissipation that took place in the Gasthaus on the top of the Brocken, ending with the incident of two intoxicated youths

22. Samuel Taylor Coleridge (1772–1834) spent ten months in Germany (1798–99).

saluting the night in Ossianic language before an open cupboard which they mistook for a window. There is also a romantic description of his meeting with a beautiful young woman with ostrich feathers in her hat, on the observation tower. From this account I was expecting to find a little more liveliness on the top of the Brocken than there actually was. It was the height of the tourist season, and although there was a large number of students and schoolboys, they were orderly and well behaved. There was no sign of dissipation or even of the high spirits that the loftiness of the situation might have been hoped to engender. The rest of the crowd was composed of bourgeois families all very placid and cow-like.

After a while we were rejoined by the Müllers. Onkel Peter was a little irritated by the triumphant smugness resulting from the energies of their ascent on foot ("we did it in an hour and a half") and he was still further irritated by the food in the Gasthaus which was not very good.

However, the view from the top of the Brocken was really magnificent, the most grandiose expanse of country I had ever seen. One might have believed that the contemplation of so immense and completely circular a view would have led thoughtful people from time immemorial to guess that the earth was round. It is strange how slow the world has been in the past to solve the riddles of the universe. Perhaps it was just as well, for now the world is getting a little too quick in doing so for general convenience.

The sky was overcast with clouds but the country below was bathed in the most brilliant sunshine in which the little towns and villages scattered over the whole vast expanse stood out in minutest detail.

"Quite a Wagnerian scene," said the Frau Först-meister, unbending a little to culture, and Onkel Peter snorted.

Baedeker assures us that the towns of Magdeburg, Erfurt, Gotha, Cassel, Hanover, Brunswick, can be seen on a clear day, adding with Baedekerian caution:

"unclouded horizon rare." However, there was such a crowd round the telescope that I hadn't the patience to await my turn and find out if this was true.

Heine says that the Brocken is a typically German institution. No doubt it is. The panorama for all its magnificence had something about it that was a little too well organized, a little too symmetrical. There was a touch of regimentation about it. All the same it was a glorious sight. It was with such a panorama as this, I thought, that the Devil must have tempted Our Saviour. A dictator perched on the summit of the Brocken might well feel that he had a thorough command of the situation and be encouraged to take advantage of it.

On the way down we visited the Hexen-altar, a place where the witches were supposed to dance on Walpürgisnacht. By this time Onkel Peter was thoroughly out of temper, and he enquired maliciously of his sister if the associations of the place made her feel she wanted to dance. For my part I didn't feel as if the spot was at all suggestive of witches' revels. It was all too respectable and looked as if it had been tidied up by municipal inspectors. No witch could dance with much abandon in the midst of notice boards and neat wooden railings.

The return journey by train was very tedious, and everyone was a little weary. I noticed that in the railway carriage the Frau Förstmeister sat bolt upright and never once leaned back. When I complimented her on her physical endurance she said that her father had brought her up to believe that to lean back or loll was effeminate. It seemed to me a little unreasonable that women should be denied an occasional lapse of effeminacy, but I supposed it was all part of the Bismarckian "blood and iron" policy.

Ernst and Heinrich went off to their cadet school. They wrote ecstatic letters to their parents about it and begged earnestly that I should be persuaded to come and see the place. As they had no particular affection for me—I could only imagine that they thought it would be a good thing for an Englishman to get a glimpse of German military efficiency. As an inducement Ernst wrote to me that perhaps I might have the privilege of seeing the young princes but, in order not to raise my hopes too much he added: "Vielleicht auch nicht" (and perhaps not).

The atmosphere of the Försthaus was decidedly more agreeable after Ernst and Heinrich had left.

I continued my peripatetic rambles with Onkel Peter. One afternoon as we were sitting on a bench in the glade known as the Philosopher's Walk, I saw approaching us two very pretty girls dressed in light flowered muslin. From their elegance, their un-German appearance, I realized at once that they couldn't be any of the local inhabitants. In these Grimm's Fairy Tale surroundings they might have been a couple of enchanted princesses. As they drew nearer I heard that they were speaking English. I stared at them and they stared at me. But maidenly discretion got the better of them. They passed on and disappeared into the wood.

Onkel Peter was as much moved by this ravishing apparition as I had been.

That evening at supper I mentioned the incident to the Frau Förstmeister. Her face clouded and she said rather acidly: "I had heard that there was an English family staying at the Gasthaus in Immenthal." Afterwards she said to me: "I trust you will make no attempt to get to know these people. I do not fancy that your parents would desire it. You must remember that you have come here to speak only German."

This manifestation of anxiety on the part of his sister did not escape Onkel Peter's notice. It aroused his puckish instincts, and on the following day as we set out for our walk, he said: "Let us go and call on the English family at Immenthal."

When we got to the inn we were told that the English lady was ill in bed, but that the two young Fräulein were there if we should by any chance care to see them. It was precisely the young Fräulein that we cared to see, and Onkel Peter sent in his visiting card. The young Fräulein appeared with such alacrity that

I suspected they had been watching us from their windows.

I had been a little afraid lest, seen at close quarters, they might prove to be less attractive than they had appeared to be in the romantic atmosphere of the sylvan glade. But I was not disappointed. There was no doubt that they were extremely pretty. They were alike in looks. One could easily see that they were sisters. They both had dark hair and fair complexions. They were about sixteen and seventeen. The elder was the prettier of the two, but she looked very fragile and delicate. The younger sister was more robust and had a livelier colour. Their names were Mary and Evelyn. Their family name was Lysaght.

When Onkel Peter expressed his regret at hearing that their mother was ill, they said: "Oh, she's not ill, she's merely resting. She can do anything she likes when she wants to."

From other things they said of their mother I gathered the impression that she might be a rather tiresome woman.

They said that they were very glad we had come to see them. They found the place rather too quiet and were beginning to be a little bored. However they were shortly going on to Hanover. That, they had heard, was a very nice place, and there were a lot of English people there.

I felt that I would have to make the most of the remaining time, and arranged to come and see them again very soon. It seemed a little inhospitable not to have invited them to the Försthaus but that, of course, was out of the question.

On the way back I implored Onkel Peter to say nothing to the Frau Förstmeister of this escapade. He promised that he would not, but added, with a glint of satisfaction: "She is bound to get to know about it sooner or later."

Having left behind him this little legacy of annoyance for his sister, Onkel Peter left shortly afterwards for Berlin.

I was saddened by his departure, but there was to be some compensation for it in the new company I had acquired. I had become quite fond of Onkel Peter. He was the first German I had got to know at all intimately and he had made me realise that there might be, after all, some Germans who could be quite nice. Nevertheless, strangely enough, I never saw him again, nor did I ever make any serious attempts to do so. When one is young it is difficult to maintain contact with people from whom one is separated by circumstances, especially when those people are older and of a different nationality. Besides there is such a constant onrush of new experiences that former ones are quickly crowded out and become obliterated. It is only in later years that they tend to creep back into one's memory as pale ghosts from the past. I have often wondered what became of Onkel Peter. If he lived on into the Nazi period he may, I fear, have come to a bad end. With his independent, epicurean temperament, his mocking outspokenness, he was not the type of man that the Nazis would have accepted very cheerfully. It is possible that his sister who, even in those earlier days, had the makings of a Nazi, might have managed to save him from persecution—but it is more probable that she would have denounced him.

After Onkel Peter went away I used to visit the two girls nearly every afternoon. As they didn't care very much about taking long or even short walks we went and sat in the woods or remained in the courtyard of the inn.

Although they were very charming young ladies, they compared a little unfavourably with the two Hervey girls. They were prettier no doubt, but they were neither witty nor intelligent. Frivolity was the keynote of their character. They reminded me of Lydia and Kitty in *Pride and Prejudice*.[23] They were passionately interested in young men, and they never ceased talking about all the "boys" they knew. The conviction grew on me that if I were to see them in the company of a lot of young men, I should like them considerably less than I did.

23. Jane Austen (1775–1817), *Pride and Prejudice* (1813).

Apart from this, there was something else about them that prevented me from bestowing on them my whole-hearted affection. When I eventually met their mother I discovered the cause of my inhibition. Mrs. Lysaght confirmed the suspicion that had been growing on me that they quite definitely belonged to the middle classes. The girls had been sent to a good finishing school and had managed to acquire a certain veneer of refinement, but the mother had had no such advantages. She aped rather pathetically what she believed to be the manners of the aristocracy, but she was betrayed by her accent, her appearance and her general outlook. She must have been quite pretty when she was young. Now she had relapsed into a middle-aged rather flabby vulgarity. She was over-dressed with a spurious smartness and resembled one of the bedizened elderly women one sees sitting about in the lounges of expensive hotels, or presiding over a supper table at a charity ball. She seemed to be under the impression that illness was fashionable. "I am not at all strong," she said to me. "My health is a constant worry to me. And my daughter Mary takes after me. She is not at all strong you know. I sometimes fear she may be consumptive. We think of going to St. Moritz this year. It's a very nice place I'm told and a lot of very smart people go there." I knew that it would be impossible to introduce the Lysaghts to my mother. Still less to invite them to Althrey. After the disaster of Marston's visit it would be inadvisable to try my mother with Mrs. Lysaght.

Here the fastidious reader will undoubtedly set me down as a snob—and with some justification. However it was difficult in those days for anyone brought up by nurses, governesses, with the final touch of a public school, not to be, in some measure, a snob. I was apt to be put off quite charming people by a peculiar accent and manners suggestive of their not being "quite the thing."

Nevertheless, for the time being, the society of the two girls was a source of considerable pleasure to me.

It had, besides, all the allurement of forbidden fruit. Although I had said nothing to the Frau Förstmeister about my friendly relations with the Lysaght girls I had a shrewd suspicion that she knew about it. I don't know who had given me away. It may have been the servants or one of the village folk.

The idyll was terminated by the departure of the Lysaght family for Hanover. Our parting was of the tenderest, and we promised to correspond regularly. The letters I received from the girls were concerned entirely with the young Englishmen they were meeting in Hanover. The place seemed to them a veritable paradise. After a while the letter-writing ceased.

Many years later Mary Lysaght came into my life again. She married an elderly naval man, a friend of my father, a rather remarkable figure, whose daring and fantastic exploits recounted to me in my childhood had made of him a sort of legendary hero. Of his feats of prowess the one that had most impressed me had been a descent he made in a parachute. Being a rather massively built man he had sought to diminish his weight by putting on silk tights. The parachute crashed through a tree and deposited him in a clergyman's garden. The amazement of the cleric at finding a huge bleeding silk-clad figure sprawling in one of his flowerbeds may be imagined.

Advancing years seemed in no way to have impaired his adventurous spirit and poor Mary, who had a delicate constitution, must have been unable to bear the strain, for after a couple of years of a rather too exciting married life, she died.

That I now entered into a period of the blackest depression cannot wholly be attributed to the fact that I was left alone with the Müllers. It is true that after enjoying the gay companionship of the Lysaghts and the more intellectual pleasures of Onkel Peter's conversation, their society was, to say the least of it, inadequate. My daily lessons with the Frau Förstmeister continued at the same dead level of dreariness, and I was made aware that she was not over-pleased about my having consorted with the Lysaghts. The Förstmeister was occupied the whole day with his forestal duties and had but little time for me. I was compelled to fall back on nature. I took my solitary walks in the woods where I had formerly been with Onkel Peter, and I passed sadly by the now deserted inn. At night I looked out on to the moonlit garden, trying in vain to feel poetical in the manner of Heine. I became a prey to morbid introspection in which there revolved a pessimistic review of my character, and panic about the examination which I was sure I should never succeed in passing. I felt that I was incapable of working hard at subjects in which I lacked the moral fortitude to force myself to be interested. I was convinced that I should never do any good in the world, that I was a useless member of society and might as well not exist. Music and literature no longer afforded me any solace. Even the score of *Don Juan* and the volume of *Zarathustra* had utterly lost their magic. In this black nightmare all the old strictures of the headmaster of Elmley cropped up again and revived once more my self-consciousness at being bad at games. I was sure that Mr. Gambril's opinion would be endorsed by the Förstmeister.[24] I didn't see the possibility of my ever taking any pleasure in life again. I was in fact suffering from a bad attack of accidie.

Accidie is, I believe, no longer accounted a deadly sin, but that doesn't make it any the less difficult to bear. Neither medical science nor psychiatry has been successful in resolving the problems of what causes it or how it may be cured. Although it is often started by some adverse experience, some mental shock, it persists when the original cause has disappeared. It is impossible to be convinced that one is being unreasonable. A sort of negative reason establishes itself and rules supreme.

24. Gambril was the headmaster of Elmley School (actually Cheam) described in Berners's *First Childhood* (1934).

Having suffered from long spells of accidie during my life, I have found that the simplest and most effective cure for it is a complete change of scene. Old-fashioned doctors, in pre-Freudian days, used to recommend for certain nervous ailments "a sea voyage," and I think they were on the right tack. I knew that I was leaving the Harz and going to Weimar at the end of September—in about a month's time—but the mere prospect of a change did nothing to ease my condition and, until it actually took place, I gained no relief.

WEIMAR

Weimar stood for a slight triumph in the matter of domestic independence. I myself had suggested to my mother that I should go there, and she had put forward no objections to my doing so. An Eton friend of mine, Martin Locksley, had written to me that he was going to a family in Weimar in the autumn and proposed that I should join him there.

My mother in any case had been averse to my staying on in the Harz during the winter months. She had an idea that it might be damp. My description of the Försthaus and the association of forests had aroused her apprehensions. As a general rule her apprehensions were liable to be a bit of a nuisance and to interfere with my scheme of life, but now they fitted in with it perfectly. And so, at the end of September, to Weimar I went.

Professor Zimmermann lived in the Henss Strasse, a street that lay on the very edge of the town. The outskirts of Weimar were very unlike those of Dresden. The environment was pleasant and countrified. There were no new houses in the process of construction, no untidy allotment grounds, no half-made streets. The Professor's house stood alone in the midst of gardens filled with fruit trees and flowers. It was a little like the Försthaus, a long low building with espaliered pear trees on the walls. A country house, in fact, an outpost of rurality in a town that in itself was not aggressively urban in character.

The family consisted of the Herr Professor, his wife and daughter. The Herr Professor was the personification of the traditional idea of a German professor. He was bald, had a walrus moustache and wore very large spectacles. His face was covered with scars, relics of the duels of his university days. He was a smaller, less bulky edition of Onkel Peter plus the scars and a moustache. His wife was a gentle little woman who looked like a parrot—a nice benevolent parrot, not one of those cross elderly birds who nip your finger to the bone. She was a homely, comfortable person who liked everything around her to be homely and comfortable. She greeted me by taking hold of both my hands and saying: "Willkommen in der neuen Pension" (Welcome to the new Pension).

The daughter Ilse was a pleasantly cow-like young woman of about thirty whose rather lymphatic appearance was redeemed by a distinctly humorous twinkle in her eyes. She had dark, smooth hair and a sallow complexion. Her expression was kindly and cheerful. With a little trouble she could have made herself look quite attractive.

The rest of the household consisted of my friend Martin Locksley and two middle-aged spinsters, Miss Macpherson and Miss Holmes. Miss Macpherson was Scotch. She was large, gaunt and rather ungainly. She had sparse, iron-grey hair, and her nose was monumental. She was dressed in a roughish tweed coat and skirt. She had decided opinions and a very heavy tread.

Miss Holmes was younger and rather plump. Her manner was extremely jaunty. It contrasted a little incongruously with her prim Victorian exterior. She was like one of those slang words in inverted commas that crop up so surprisingly in the pages of Henry James.

A description of Martin Locksley's personality will be given in the course of my story. It may suffice at this point to say that he was tall, dark and rather good-looking. His appearance was slightly effeminate in the way that quite a number of young Englishmen have a slightly effeminate appearance that is in reality misleading. However, there was no tiresome ultra-manliness about him. He was gentle, intelligent and cultivated. Like myself he was destined for the diplomatic service.

I must not omit to mention the Zimmermanns' dog, a curious-looking mongrel, a conglomeration of many breeds. When I asked the Frau Professor what sort of a dog it was she answered with a note of pride: "Das ist ein Luxus-hund"—a luxury dog.

Each member of the Pension had a bedroom and a sitting-room next to it. The house was furnished for the most part in a rather tasteless fashion, but there was a great air of comfort everywhere. Gemütlichkeit was the prevailing note both of the house and its owners. We had meals in a long room on the ground floor with French windows opening on to the garden. In this room we also sat in the evenings. It was known as the Wohnzimmer. There was a drawing room, also on the ground floor, but it was only used for special occasions, for the reception of people whom the Frau Professor wanted to impress or of people she feared might bore us.

My depression had by now almost completely vanished. I had shed a good deal of it in the train. That awful nervous sensation of a windmill going round in one's heart (known in later years as angst) had ceased. On the following day my cure was completed by the weather. It was a marvellous autumn day. There was bright sunshine and the blue sky was heaped with mountainous white clouds. In the air was perfect stillness. Not a leaf stirred and the "autumn tints" were in full swing. Never before had I seen so gorgeous a display of scarlet yellow and pale green. The temperature was still summery, but there was a healthy exhilarating nip in the air. Martin and I walked up a road that led from the house into the open country. On the way he pointed out to me a house where Nietzsche had lived and where he had died a few years ago. It was now inhabited by his sister Frau Forster-Nietzsche. I was unaware that Nietzsche had lived in Weimar. Baedeker had not yet got as far as Nietzsche and didn't include him among the Weimar celebrities. To find his house here seemed to add to the attractions of the place. Martin didn't share my enthusiasm for Nietzsche, nor did the Zimmermann family. Fräulein Ilse said that once, passing the house, she had seen Nietzsche himself looking out of the window. At that time he had already entered on his final stage of insanity. She said that although it was growing dusk she could observe his face quite distinctly through the glass. His eyes, she said, were terrible, and the general effect had been "unheimlich" (weird).

To anyone unacquainted with Weimar it would be difficult to convey an adequate impression of its charm. The town was not in the least sensational like Heidelberg, Hildesheim or Würzburg. The guidebook says: "Weimar retains much of its medieval character," but I think this must be intended as a sop for the romantic. It is true that there were a few medieval buildings, but they were discreetly tucked away, and the general aspect of the place was eighteenth century in character. The atmosphere was one of amiable placidity, of the comfortable culture that, one imagines, must have prevailed almost everywhere in Germany at the end of the eighteenth up to the middle of the nineteenth century in spite of the Napoleonic wars. That this atmosphere should still persist in Weimar was due no doubt to the fact that the Grand Dukes had always discouraged industrial development, but above all to the spirit of Goethe that still hovered over the place. Associations with Goethe are everywhere. Goethe designed the Grand Ducal Schloss and the charming "English Park" on either side of the little river Ilm. The Theatre is the theatre of *Wilhelm Meister* and Goethe ran it in its heyday. There was the Goethe-Haus in the town and his Garden House in the park, and Goethe set up the curious little stone altar with a serpent coiling round the base in a shrubbery overlooking the park. In Weimar Goethe was ever-present.

I have not been to Weimar since the days of the Weimar Republic and cannot tell if and to what extent the pleasant atmosphere of the place may have been polluted. But I like to think that Goethe's personality is strong enough to have resisted any encroachments of modernity and that Weimar is one of those towns like Vienna or Rome whose flavour no architectural disfigurement, no change of regime can wholly spoil.

Thackeray took Weimar as his model for the little town of Pumpernickel in *Vanity Fair*, where Becky and Amelia effected their reconciliation.[25] When Thackeray lived there the Court seems to have been far more lively and hospitable than it was in my day. He speaks of an endless succession of court balls, concerts and receptions—a continual round of gaiety. Now the Grand Ducal Court was almost imperceptible, and if

25. William Makepeace Thackeray (1811–63), *Vanity Fair* (1847).

there were any festivities they occurred unnoticed. In Thackeray's day there were foreign ministers and ambassadors at Weimar. Now there were hardly any foreigners and only an English Chaplain and an American Consul.

The present Grand Duke and Grand Duchess were very quiet people. There was a current legend that the Grand Duchess was unhappily married, having been forced by the Kaiser against her will to marry the Grand Duke. I saw them occasionally walking together in the Park. They were both quite young and nice looking. The Grand Duke didn't give the impression of a tyrant nor did the Grand Duchess look like an unhappily married woman.

It soon became evident to me that I was going to be as happy in Weimar as I had been at Résenlieu.[26] No member of the household was quite as wonderful

26. Berners, *The Château de Résenlieu* (Turtle Point Press and Helen Marx Books, 2000).

as Madame O'Kerrins nor as charming as Mademoiselle Henriette, but there were other compensations. In the place of the French elegance and the idyllically pastoral atmosphere of Résenlieu there was German comfort and cosiness and there were the many amenities of Weimar: the Hof Theater, where both operas and plays were given, an excellent book shop, several antique shops, a music shop where I could hire a piano for my sitting room, and a Konditorei that supplied all manner of cakes and sweets, delicious coffee, chocolate and ices. All this was a matter of five minutes walk from the Henss Strasse. A few minutes' walk in the opposite direction took one into the open country. Thus a small radius contained the pleasures of both the town and the country.

I had lessons every morning with the Professor. His teaching was perhaps more enjoyable than useful for the purposes of the examination. He concentrated entirely on literature and refrained from plaguing me with out-of-the way political and commercial phrases, all the things that made the idea of the examination so repulsive to me. As I have said elsewhere, pleasure always had a relaxing effect on my sense of duty, and the prospect of the examination ceased for a time to trouble me. I hardly gave it a thought.

As befitted an inhabitant of Weimar the Professor was a great Goethe enthusiast. He made me study *Faust* and helped me in the more difficult passages. He also gave me Eckermann's *Conversations with Goethe* to read. This book I enjoyed thoroughly. As the books I read had a considerable influence on me and coloured the atmosphere of the place and the period in which I read them, it will not be amiss, at this point, to say a few words about *Eckermann*. It is one of the books I constantly re-read, as much for Goethe's wise pontifical utterances as for the passages of unconscious humour of which the book is full. The worthy Eckermann, so devoted, so painstaking, seems never to be aware that the Divine Goethe is occasionally pulling his leg. And Goethe, while loath to offend his enthusiastic recorder, appears at moments to be growing a little impatient. For instance, when Eckermann parades his bird-lore with evident satisfaction at knowing more about birds than Goethe. A comment of Goethe's, after a long and tedious bird story about two young wrens and some robins cannot, I think, but be ironic in intention. The story ends thus: "How great was my surprise when I found in the nest my two young wrens which had established themselves very comfortably and allowed themselves to be fed by the two old robins. 'That is one of the best bird stories I have ever heard,' said Goethe."

Goethe, however, managed to get his own back with elaborate expositions of his Theory of Colours and would say to Eckermann: "I shall tell you no more at present. You must find out the rest for yourself."

There was one touching example of Eckermann's solicitude. He and Goethe were picnicking at Berka.

"Goethe cut a partridge and gave me one half. I ate standing up and walking about. Goethe had seated himself on a heap of stones. The coldness of the stones on which the night dew was still resting might, I thought, be dangerous for him, and I expressed my anxiety. However, Goethe assured me that it would do him no harm, and I felt quite tranquil regarding it as a new token of his inward strength."

Among other curiosities there was a strange account of Schiller's rotten apples that had an almost Freudian flavour. Goethe visited Schiller and, finding him absent, seated himself at Schiller's writing table. Almost at once he began to "feel queer." "At first I did not know to what cause to ascribe my wretched and unusual state—until I discovered that a dreadful odour issued from a drawer. I opened it and found to my amazement that it was full of rotten apples. His wife told me that the drawer was always filled with rotten apples because the smell was beneficial to Schiller and he could not work or live without it."

The book, on the whole, presented the great Goethe in a very amiable light and gave a pleasant picture of German life as it was in those days. It was one of the books that, together with those of Heine, Jean Paul, Hoffmann and other writers of that period, contributed to inspire me with an affection for Germany that even two wars and the Nazis have not entirely killed.

It seems difficult to believe that national characteristics which are largely dependent on geography should utterly disappear. Perhaps someday the country will return to conditions in which its more lovable aspects may be able to assert themselves. It was after the reunification of Germany that she began to make a nuisance of herself. It looks as if Bismarck and Pan-Germanism were at the root of the trouble. Goethe may have had a prophetic vision of what was going to happen. "Whence is Germany great," he said to Eckermann, "but by the admirable culture of the people, which equally pervades all parts of the kingdom? But does not this proceed from the various seats of government? Do not these foster and support it? Suppose that for centuries past there had been in Germany only the two capitals Berlin and Vienna or only one of these. I would like to see how it would have fared with German culture, or with the general well-being that goes with culture. Dresden, Munich, Hanover, Stuttgart are great and brilliant, their effect on the culture and well-being of Germany are incalculable. Would they have their same influence if they lost their sovereignty and became incorporated in a great German kingdom as provincial towns? I see every reason to doubt it."[27]

In the course of reading Eckermann I discovered the sources of a good many of the Professor's tenets. He said to me one day: "Miss Macpherson tells me her God moves in a mysterious way. I say to her: Don't try to fathom Divine Mysteries. Endeavour only to

---

27. Berners crossed out this paragraph in the typescript.

cope with them. If it comes on to rain, don't ask yourself why it rains but get your umbrella."

Goethe had said: "Man is not born to solve the problems of the universe but to find out where the problems apply."

The Professor and Miss Macpherson had frequent discussions on theology, a subject Miss Macpherson had been studying. As Miss Macpherson's command of German was not very secure, these discussions occasionally lapsed into English. The Professor was in the habit of referring to the Holy Ghost as the "holy goat," which very much distressed Miss Macpherson. She complained to me: "I do wish the Professor wouldn't keep on saying 'the holy goat.' I always correct him and I am beginning to think he does it deliberately just to annoy me."

Miss Macpherson took her religion very seriously. I was never able to discover what her religious views really were. She seemed by nature Calvinistic but at times she appeared to lean towards Catholicism. In any case she was always very decided in the expression of her opinions, and she was violently in favour of drastic action. "If I were an absolute monarch," she used to say, "I would have people who do this or that (whatever it was she disapproved of) beheaded."

She was in the habit of writing "strong letters" to the newspapers and I was told that when the war of 1914 broke out she sent a telegram to the Pope. "Pope. Vatican, Rome. Stop war. Macpherson."

Although Miss Macpherson and her friend Miss Holmes seemed to be on the friendliest terms, there were occasional clashes between the former's rude authority and the latter's perky prevarication. Their quarrels flared up and died down again with equal rapidity. I once heard Miss Macpherson shout, as she flounced out of Miss Holmes's room: "Very well then, you can stew in your own juice!" I don't know how long Miss Holmes was left to stew in her own juice. At supper-time they were quite friendly again.

Miss Macpherson was temperamentally incapable

of doing anything quietly. She slammed doors or shut them in such a way that the whole house trembled, and when she came downstairs it was like a herd of cattle descending. Once when she ran after me in the street I had the impression that I was being pursued by a carthorse.

She and the Professor got on very well together. He was always very playful with her and teased her a good deal, which she rather enjoyed. He once went so far as to tickle her. The spectacle of the gaunt spinster being tickled by the Professor is one that I shall never forget.

So you see there was plenty of fun and merriment in the Pension, and sometimes towards the end of meals when everyone was stoked up with food and drink, what with the Professor's bellowing and Miss Macpherson's harsh screams, the noise was almost intolerable. Miss Holmes and the Frau Professor made less noise than the rest of the party. Miss Holmes's perkiness was birdlike in its quality. Her chirpings and twitterings were drowned in the general rumpus, while the Frau Professor confined herself to smiling and pressing more food on everyone.

As long as the fine autumn weather continued, Martin and I used to go for long walks together, exploring the country round Tiefurt and Berka. Sometimes we went by train to more distant places, Jena, Gotha, Eisenach and walked part of the way back. It might seem natural that, being alike in tastes and disposition, we should, in the course of these excursions, have come to know one another very well. But even at the end of a couple of months our relationship had not progressed beyond a certain degree of mild intimacy. That we were not more in one another's confidence was, perhaps, my fault rather than his. As a result of having been an only child and of having formed at an early age a habit of solitude, I never seemed able to establish anything but a rather superficial relationship with my friends—even with Deniston whom I had so passionately adored. Moreover, being always a little doubtful about my character, I instinctively surrounded it with a protective barrier to prevent people from prying into it too closely and discovering its deficiencies.

In contemporary novels I had read of young men who were in the habit of discussing in the profoundest manner their souls, their religion and their plans for bettering the world. I was rather glad that I didn't know any such young men. Martin was certainly not one of them. He didn't give me the impression of thinking very profoundly about anything, except perhaps about his work for the diplomatic examinations and his religion. He was religious and I, who was not, often found it strange that anyone so intelligent should hold some of the beliefs he appeared to do. However, I felt no inclination to argue with him on the subject. Argument between sceptics and believers I had already discovered to be an unprofitable business.

In ordinary everyday matters Martin was a good

deal more self-assured than I was. He seemed able to settle any problems that confronted him promptly and calmly. I always had difficulty in making up my mind. Indecision was a defect of character that I had no doubt inherited from my mother.

Martin had neither the elegant worldliness of Deniston nor the heroic glamour of Milward, but he had a kindlier nature than either of them and was more dependable, and he was quite personable enough to satisfy my aesthetic requirements. He shared my love for books, pictures and music. He had a quiet taste in literature. He preferred Jane Austen to any other writer, and one of his favourite books was *Cranford*. He preferred classical music to modern music.

Our greatest bond of union was the similarity in our sense of humour. We both of us enjoyed nonsense and whenever conversation showed signs of becoming acrimonious or too serious, nonsense would come to the rescue. We were both perhaps a little priggish in that unconscious humour both in books and in daily life (of which there occurred a good many instances in the Pension) appealed to us more than straightforward wit and humour. We were amused by innocent practical jokes. One evening when Miss Macpherson and Miss Holmes, who were ardent halma[28] players, had left the room for a moment, we gummed down one of the pawns to the halma board so that when Miss Macpherson, who was winning, attempted to pick it up, the whole board collapsed in confusion. The row that ensued was terrific.

Martin and I had invented a sort of card game that was played with the Zimmermanns' family photograph album. It consisted in detaching the photographs from their paper frames, shuffling them and dealing them face downwards. The ugliest took the trick. There were two aunts who caused such endless discussion as to which was the uglier of the two that

28. Halma—a board game like Chinese chequers.

they had to be eliminated from the pack. Of course the game could only be played with safety when the Zimmermann family were absent from the house. One day Fräulein Ilse, who we thought was out, came suddenly into the room. With great presence of mind Martin swept the album and all the photographs on to the floor and we made a great business of picking them up and restoring them to the album. Fräulein Ilse looked a little suspicious, but I am sure she can have had no idea as to what we had really been up to.

I used to go two or three times a week to the Hof Theater, generally with Martin, sometimes with the Zimmermanns. Never have I experienced such easy and agreeable conditions of theatre-going as in Weimar. The price of the seats was incredibly low and there was never any difficulty about getting them. On the evenings when we went to the theatre we had a sort of high-tea (known as Jause) about an hour before the performance, which was generally at seven o'clock. The theatre, although fairly large, had a pleasant atmosphere of cosiness and intimacy, and the variety of plays and operas performed was extensive. The plays were generally classical favourites; *Minne von Barnhelm* (Lessing), *Kabale und Liebe* (Schiller) etc., and there was a preponderance of plays by Schiller and Goethe—*Wallenstein, Die Räuber, Maria Stuart, Torquato Tasso, Iphigenia* and *Clavigo*.

In front of the theatre there were the statues of Schiller and Goethe clasping one another by the hand. I remember, at the time of the Eulenberg scandal, seeing a caricature of these statues in *Simplicissimus* in which Schiller was saying to Goethe: "Let go my hand, Wolfgang, here comes Dr. Magnus Hirschfeld."[29]

An opera that was frequently performed was

29. *Simplicissimus* was a German satirical magazine started in 1896. Magnus Hirschfeld (1868–1935) was a well-known writer on sexual pathology who was in the habit of attributing homosexual tendencies to many of the great figures of the past. [Berners's note.]

Massenet's *Werther*. I have not heard it since then and am not sure if it would appeal to me now. At that time I thought it enchanting. The music seemed to me to render perfectly the poetical environment of the story. Another opera that was often given was *Saint Elizabeth* by Liszt, another local celebrity. Of this I can only remember a chorus of Crusaders who tramped round the stage shouting "Gott will es" and a scene in which Saint Elizabeth, taking a basket of loaves to the famine-stricken peasants, was surprised by her husband, a cruel tyrant temperamentally opposed to charity. He asked her what was in the basket. She said: "Roses." He snatched the covering from the basket and lo! roses there were. I asked Miss Macpherson if it were all right for saints to tell lies. She said: "Saints can do anything they damned well like." All the same I couldn't help thinking that it would have been better if Saint Elizabeth had had the courage of her convictions and had brazened the matter out.

The days passed peacefully and pleasantly. In spite

of the regularity of the day's programme, it never grew monotonous. In the morning, after my lesson with the Professor, I used to walk into the town, inspect the book shop and the music shop, visit the antiquaries, take tickets for the theatre or drink coffee or chocolate at the Konditorei. In the afternoon I went for a walk with Martin and worked for an hour or two, which generally meant reading *Faust* or Eckermann. In the evening I either went to the theatre or stayed at home with the family.

Not a very exciting programme, you will say. However, in reaction to the enforced activities of school life and of home life as well, I enjoyed, as I had enjoyed at Résenlieu, a routine of peace and quiet in which my life was simplified and there was no necessity to live in a perpetual state of defensive extemporisation.

The Zimmermanns were socially inclined. They had a good many friends who were continually "looking in" on them. None of them were exceptionally interesting. They were just nice, amiable people. Their conversation was generally about local gossip and the servant problem which is an enthralling topic in every country. I longed to make the acquaintance of Nietzsche's sister who lived only a hundred yards or so from the Henss Strasse. I didn't know at that time that Nietzsche had referred to her in one of his letters as "eine dumme Gans." Even if I had, I should have still liked to have met her. But the Zimmermanns didn't know her. Nor was their interest in Nietzsche sufficient to inspire them with the wish to do so.

My ambition to compose a symphonic poem had been revived by a concert I went to at which Richard Strauss's *Don Quixote* had been played. The subject I chose was nothing less than Dante's *Inferno*, and beyond inventing an opening theme with which I was not particularly pleased I didn't progress very far with it. The Zimmermanns were always ready to welcome any signs of talent in the inmates of the Pension. They continually asked me how I was getting on with it, and I was loath to confess that I was not getting on with it at all.

My musical activities were cut short by a sudden and violent craze for Ibsen.[30] There was to be a performance of *Ghosts* to which Martin and I decided to go. Fräulein Ilse refused to accompany us, but she whetted our appetite by saying that the play was "schauerlich" (morbid) and altogether disagreeable. *Ghosts* was not considered to be sufficiently conventional to be performed at the Hof Theater and had to be given in a hall on the outskirts of the town. On this little makeshift stage the play had all the attributes of an amateur performance. But the acting was anything but amateur. An actress called Luise Dumont took the part of Frau Alving. Her interpretation of the role was the most perfect I have ever seen, not excluding that of Duse. The play made such an impression on me that I could think and talk of nothing else for

30. Henrik Ibsen (1828–1906), *Ghosts* (1881).

days afterwards. Miss Holmes, who went to see it on the following night, said that it had given her the collywobbles. No other plays of Ibsen were acted in Weimar, and I had to content myself with reading them. I read *Rosmersholm*, *The Lady from the Sea*, *John Gabriel Borkman*, and *Hedda Gabler*, which were the only ones I could get at the time. The result of my Ibsen craze was that I was smitten with the idea of writing a play myself in the manner of Ibsen, and started at once to do so. The subject of my play was the story of a married woman who fell in love with another man, upon which her husband went mad. She was unable to get rid of him, and her lover left her. Not a very ingenious plot and one which, I foresaw, was going to land me in difficulties about the marriage laws of which I knew nothing. I wrote the first act and read it to Martin who was very kind about it. He said to me shortly afterwards: "I don't think I could ever write a play. I'm not creative. You see people are either creative or receptive and I know that I am only receptive." Although I was sure that his remark was not aimed at me in particular, it caused me to ponder. I wondered if I, perhaps, were only receptive. The thought was discouraging and, after that, the play, for one reason and another, began to languish.

Miss Macpherson and Miss Holmes used often to speak of the dislike of the Germans for England. This surprised and disturbed me. In Dresden, it is true, I had from time to time noticed evidences of this dislike, but I imagined that it was only directed against the English who were actually in Dresden— and for this, I thought, there might perhaps be some excuse. In Weimar I had experienced nothing of the kind. Everyone seemed friendly and particularly amiable to the English.

At Résenlieu, while the Boer War was in progress, I had come across manifestations of anglophobia in the town, and I was under the impression that the French hated the English more than the Germans did. So, when I was assured that the Germans disliked the

English, I thought that it might be a characteristic of all nations that they should dislike other nations— except of course in the case of the English who were above such pettiness.

I should no doubt have been more concerned if I had read the political articles in the German newspapers or the more modern German history books, in which aspersions are continually cast on the part played by England in world politics, or had I probed more diligently into the opinions of my German friends.

However, I had the habit of turning a blind eye on things I didn't wish to see. There are certain advantages to our peace of mind in being unobservant or indifferent. We at least remain innocent and happy until the crash comes. And when the crash does come, it is just as bad for those who had foreseen it as for those who hadn't. The provisions taken by the wise are only in rare cases successful. It seems to be an argument in favour of fatalism that those who foresee things, in the matter of politics at any rate, are generally unwilling or unable to do very much to remedy matters, and there is scant consolation in being in a position to say: "I told you so."

I am all on the side of the Foolish Virgins, and if their story had been told elsewhere than in Holy Scripture, I have always believed that their fate might have been less disastrous. And that if the bridegroom had been at all a decent fellow they must have been more attractive to him than their wiser sisters. (The Ant and the Grasshopper.)

Christmas was approaching. In a book of memoirs Maurice Baring has said: "Christmas is the captain jewel of German domestic life. No one who has not spent a Christmas with a German family can know Germany."

It is true that Christmas is a typically German institution. Many of the features of the customary celebration of Christmas were introduced, in Victorian days, by the Prince Consort, and the season was subsequently popularised by Dickens.

A fortnight before Christmas, the festive spirit sprang into activity in Weimar. The town and the shops began to glow with all the signs of the approaching season. Christmas trees in embryo state were being sold in the market place. The confectioners, the toy shops, even the butchers' shops were decked with tinsel, frosted cotton wool and garlands of coloured paper, and were more brilliantly illuminated than usual. The faces of the citizens shone with the expression of good will to men, and even the grumpy proprietor of the music shop became blander and more disposed to try and find what you wanted.

In the Henss Strasse, cakes, sweets (in which marzipan predominated) and other delicacies were being prepared. The Frau Professor was continually hinting at surprises that were in store for us. Martin and I had never before spent Christmas in Germany, and she was particularly anxious that our first impression should be a good one.

Appropriately, a few days before Christmas, snow

fell and the setting was complete. The little town had the perfect appearance of a Christmas card, and the streets were full of children taking home Christmas trees and firewood in sledges.

On Christmas Day we all went to an afternoon service in the Stadtkirche which filled me with Christian emotion. Under the impression of the lamp-lit, decorated church, the chorales that were sung, and the fervent air of the congregation, I felt like that atheistic character in Anatole France who exclaimed when he heard the *Dies Irae* being played on the organ in the Cathedral: "Cela me fout des idées religieuses."

The Zimmermanns had prepared in secret a marvellous Christmas tree which was moved into the Wohnzimmer on Christmas Day. There were presents for all, arranged in a little bower of cotton wool ornamented with silver stars, stucco angels and glittering glass balls. The two spinsters received reproductions of Della Robbia babies, which was perhaps the Professor's idea of humour. Martin had a carved Meerschaum pipe, and I was given an elaborately bound volume of *Faust* which I still possess. I presented the Frau Professor with a Venetian glass goblet which was placed in the drawing room to be an object of admiration for distinguished visitors. The servants had a Christmas tree of their own in the kitchen and even the dog had one, hung with sausages and bones done up in ribbons.

Both meals at the Pension overflowed with Christmas cheer. The evening meal was the more sumptuous and festive of the two. We drank "Glühwein," which was a hot spiced red wine, and there was a flaming punch bowl. We all got rather drunk. Martin had produced a box of paper caps, and the Professor and the two spinsters in their caps looked like a *Capricho* of Goya attuned to Christmas.[31] There was a discordant chorus of *Heilige Nacht*. The Professor bellowed, Miss Macpherson screamed, and festivity reached the highest pitch of noise and gaiety.

31. Series of etchings by Francisco José de Goya (1746–1828).

That Christmas in Weimar was one of the passages of my youth that remained imprinted in glowing colours on my memory, and often during the periods in which we were at war with Germany, when Christmas came round it used to come back to me arousing most inappropriately a revival of affection and a feeling of nostalgic regret.